The Reluctant Artist

by Laurie Bellet

ISBN 1-891662-21-x

Torah Aura Productions • 4423 Fruitland Avenue, Los Angeles, CA 90058
(800) BE-Torah • (800) 238-6724 • (323) 585-7312 • fax (323) 585-0327
E-MAIL <misrad@torahaura.com> • Visit the Torah Aura website at
www.torahaura.com

MANUFACTURED IN UNITED STATES OF AMERICA

The Makings of a Reluctant Artist

When I was a little girl, I desperately wanted to be "good" in art. It seemed to me that my friends needed nothing more than paper and crayons to create magic! Inevitably, my mother had to break the news to me. She informed me, with gentle honesty, that I had absolutely no artistic talent.

This recollection confirms for me what I now know to be absolutely true. Any teacher, even with no artistic background, no innate skill, and no confidence can create a wonderfully meaningful classroom art program.

And that is what the projects in this book are all about.

You will find this book different than most books on this topic. These projects are not specific to any holiday nor are they uniform in their final result. Rather, these projects represent a variety of techniques. The results can be so varied that you may

designate a project for use with any topic of study.

This book invites you to expand your views of the scope of Jewish classroom art; to think beyond the typical; to see Jewish art in everyday objects and materials. Perhaps most importantly, this book will encourage you to take a risk and explore the exciting dimensions of your own creativity.

You will not find complicated techniques or exotic materials in these projects. The materials are easily available at your nearest craft retailer and the project plans guide your every step. There are, however, secrets to the success of a Reluctant Artist. I would be delighted to share them with you:

- Before presenting a project in the classroom, always do your own, from start to finish, at home. Discover the pitfalls; Plan how you will teach the technique; Learn how long it is likely to take; Figure out how to correct inevitable mistakes; Adapt the plans for your particular skills and students.

- When you make mistakes in your work, let your students know! They will respect your candor and be much more tolerant of their own efforts.

- Whenever possible, laminate your students paper projects. Lamination brightens colors and increases durability. Your students, and their parents, will be honored to know that you regard their efforts so highly.

- Photograph your students as they work on their art projects and create a bulletin board to show everyone the incredible activity in your room! Congratulate yourself whenever you view the bulletin board and send the student photos home in your report cards.

- When asked if a plate or cup is dishwasher safe, smile and remind the questioner that it is better to simply wipe family heirlooms with a damp cloth. (I learned the hard way that some dishwashers are much more aggressive than my own.)
- Try new things and accept that some projects will not work out as well as others. One particular class of students, whom I have taught for several years, votes each May as to which project was my "failure" that year. Not everyone agrees and we all laugh about it! (By the way, none of those projects appear in this book.)

Each of these project techniques has been taught in day schools, supplemental schools, high schools and summer camps. The students and campers have ranged in age from pre-schoolers to adults, representing a vast range of ability areas. Teen counselors and teaching assistants, art specialists, classroom teachers, and parents have all implemented these projects.

you can do this!

Even A Reluctant Artist Needs The Right Stuff

Every artist needs a functional palette. For the Reluctant Artist this means having a wealth of materials at the ready for you and your students to enjoy:

- X-Acto blade (You can purchase this at a craft or hardware store)
- A selection of fine-line and broad-line markers (Lakeshore's assortment is terrific)
- Sea Sponge (Purchase at the craft store; cut into pieces and dampen before use)
- "People Color"/ "Global Markers" from Lakeshore or Crayola (The greatest impediment that kids have when including people in their artwork is the skin tone)
- Mod Podge (get the biggest size possible; experiment with different finishes)
- Dot Art Paint Markers (An easy, quick and clean way to paint; they are great for making colorful Bingo/game boards.)
- Gel Pens (Accumulate these whenever you see them at 75 cents or less per pen; they help turn any writing assignment into art)
- Tacky glue/Wood glue/craft glue (for those "extra stick" projects; store the glue in baby food jars and apply with a q-tip or chop stick)

- Sharpie permanent markers
- Gold or Silver "Leafing" Markers (for those extra glitzy touches)

Be certain to keep your "studio" well stocked with:

- Wrapping paper scraps
- Greeting cards and Bar/ Bat Mitzvah invitations (great for pictures or to cut with your X-Acto knife to make small frames)
- Beads, Buttons and Bottle Caps
- Yarn
- Stickers
- Stencils
- Fabric Swatches
- Jewish Merchandise Catalogs (Please remember to purchase from those catalogs whose pictures you use so frequently!)
- Decorative paper (from scrapbook supplies or origami)
- Wallpaper books
- Hebrew newspaper
- Jewish calendars

In order to store all this great stuff you will need a healthy supply of empty baby-wipe-sized containers. Label the outside according to the contents and stack these in your cabinets so that they are quickly and clearly accessible.

Do not fret about acquiring all these fabulously useful art supplies because you can:

- Send home "Want Ads"; parents will share their treasures with you
- Post notices on synagogue and school bulletin boards or in newsletters.
- Visit "dollar" stores and close-out stores

- Watch the craft store ads and coupons (be alert to seasonal specials and stock up)
- Count on word of mouth; let people know you collect junk.

Take Note Of some Really wonderful Resources

- www.eNASCO.com: This is an inexpensive source for everything the Reluctant Artist could ever need. To request a print catalog of arts and crafts supplies, telephone 1-800-558-9595.
- www.CRAYOLA.com: A great site for project ideas and Jewish coloring patterns.
- www.SCIPLUS.com: This monthly newsprint catalog is an extraordinary source of junkyard treasures. A fantastic vendor for boxes, jars, bottles and so much more.
- www.LAKESHORELEARNING.com: The elementary catalog includes their art supplies. Locate a store near to you for inexpensive laminating and book binding.

update your Library

Your young artists will have an endless supply of starting points if your library includes the following:

- Several Siddurim
- A kid-friendly Hebrew dictionary
- A simple reference for Jewish quotes.
- A "creative lettering" book (check your scrapbooking retailer)

Plate For All Seasons And Reasons

Variation I—(Kindergarten and above)

Materials

- One glass plate per student (you may obtain these at linen stores for about $10.00/dozen)
- Simple Judaic design (sample follows on next page)
- Permanent markers (Sharpies, Speedball markers, DecoMarkers)
- Gold or silver acrylic paint (such as "Gleams" by Creamcoat)
- Scotch tape and scissors
- Sea sponge

Preparation

- Tape the paper, design face down, onto the *top*side of the plate.
- Turn the plate bottom-side up; you will be drawing on the bottom. (This way, no paint will ever be in contact with food items.)

Activity

- Using the permanent markers, trace and color the design (through the glass) directly onto the bottom of the plate. Designs can be traced onto the rim area as well as in the center. If the design contains any lettering, please see the special note below. Artistically confident students can draw freehand, but should be reminded that their design will appear reversed when the plate is turned right-side up.
- Allow sufficient time for the marker to dry completely.
- Slightly moisten the sea sponge and dab the gold or silver paint onto the bottom of the plate. You can cover as much or as little of the design as you wish; the metallic paint will appear as background when the plate is turned right-side up again.
- Twenty-four hours after painting, bake the plate for 30 minutes in a 300 degree oven.
- If the design contains any lettering or wording (recommended for students 4th grade and above) turn the paper print-side down and trace the letters or words onto the back. The words will appear as "mirror writing." Tape the reversed letters or words onto the front side of the plate and traced the reversed images. These will appear in their proper orientation when the plate is placed face up.

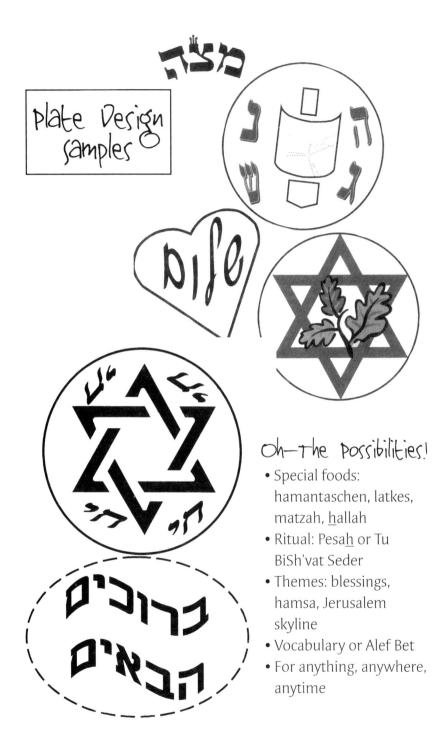

מצה

plate Design
samples

שלום

ברוכים
הבאים

Oh—the possibilities!
- Special foods: hamantaschen, latkes, matzah, hallah
- Ritual: Pesah or Tu BiSh'vat Seder
- Themes: blessings, hamsa, Jerusalem skyline
- Vocabulary or Alef Bet
- For anything, anywhere, anytime

Plate For All Seasons And Reasons

Variation 2

Materials—

- Glass plate (as in Variation 1)
- Simple (Judaic) design
- Permanent markers (as in Variation 1)
- Tissue paper (any color desired)
- Mod Podge
- Scotch tape
- Scissors
- Foam brushes

Preparation

- Tape the paper, design facedown, onto the topside of the plate.
- Turn the plate bottom-side up; you will be drawing on the bottom. (No paint will ever be in contact with food items.)

Activity

- Using the permanent markers, trace and color the design (through the glass) directly onto the bottom of the plate. Designs can be traced onto the rim area as well as in the center. If the design contains any lettering, please see the special note below. Artistically confident students can draw freehand, but should be reminded that their design will appear reversed when the plate is turned right-side up.

- *—Or—* trace and color design onto white tissue paper, then lay the white tissue, drawing-side down, onto the bottom of the plate so that the design shows through to the front of the plate.
- Allow sufficient time for the marker to dry completely.
- With a foam brush, apply a thin layer of Mod Podge over the bottom side of the plate.
- Cut or tear tissue paper and completely cover the bottom of the plate.
- Cover with a thicker layer of Mod Podge and allow to dry completely. It will be tacky for at least 24 hours.

See Variation 1 for notes on using lettering or words and for theme suggestions.

Kiddush Cups

Variation 1
(Kindergarten and up. Adults love this version!)

Materials:

- Glass goblets (bed and bath stores frequently sell for about $10 per dozen) Try to resist the impulse to use plastic. Plastic goblets are, by design, disposable.

- Tissue paper—there are many beautiful prints and colors available.

- Mod Podge or other similar finish- gloss luster, sparkle or antique

- Foam brushes

Activity:

- Paint the outside of the goblet with Mod Podge.

- Place small pieces of torn or cut tissue paper around the outside of the cup, continuing to add Mod Podge as needed to adhere the tissue pieces.

- When desired area(s) is covered, paint carefully over the tissue paper with the Mod Podge.
- Allow to dry. Paint again as desired for extra strength.

Optional:

- Use "Simulated Leading" (purchased commercially or use white glue mixed with India ink) to carefully outline or decorate tissue covered areas. This is difficult for most students under 4th grade level.
- Add a picture from a Jewish catalog to the Kiddush Cup design. Cover the picture with Mod Podge so that it becomes part of the design.

Kiddush Cup

Variation 2
(students at 5th grade level and above)

Materials:

- Glass goblets—see above
- Sharpie marker (fine)
- Permanent markers
- Simple clip art or other design (suggestions below)
- Simulated Liquid Leading
- Gold or Silver Leafing marker (optional)
- Scotch tape

Activity:

- Select clip art design (if desired); trim and tape design into the inside of the cup facing outward.
- —Or— draw a simple design and proceed as you would with clip art.
- —Or— place strips of scotch tape around the cup to create stripes or other linear designs.
- With a fine Sharpie marker, trace your design through the glass onto the outside of the goblet. If you are using scotch tape, outline the design you have created.
- Practice with the simulated leading on a piece of paper to gain control of the flow.
- Carefully trace over your design with the simulated leading.
- Allow "leading" to dry fully. (Generally, overnight is best.)

- With permanent markers or glass paint, paint inside the "leaded" design areas.
- Use metallic leafing pens as desired in distinct areas.
- Allow to dry and add additional coats as desired.

Some kind of vine

DISCOVER THE POSSIBILITIES!
using the same techniques you can create...

yahrzeit Candle Holders

Votive candle glass cups—can generally purchased at discount (approximately 50 cents apiece) during pre- and post-holiday craft store sales.

Can be done as a project in coordination with any Yizkor service, Yom HaShoah commemoration, Life Cycle curriculum.

Candlesticks

- "Close Out" stores frequently sell "crystal" candlesticks for less than $1.00 each.
- After decorating with paint or tissue, outline or fill in gaps with a gold or silver leafing marker.

Handwashing Bowls & Pitchers

- Glass pitchers and bowls are frequently in stock at "Close Out" stores and "Dollar" stores.

- Young children can trace their handprints onto white paper. The design can be minimized in the photocopier to fit the bottom of the bowl.

- Place the hand design face down in the bottom of the bowl so that it can be traced onto the bottom and sponge painted as for plates.

- This project can be completed with a hand towel. See ideas for fabric decorating on page 30.

This can be done all throughout the year or specific for Pesa<u>h</u>.

Haroset Bowl

Use design below to trace onto the bottom of bowl or around the rim.

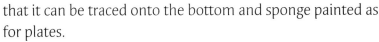

19

Puzzle Gram

(kdg and up/25 cents per project)

Materials:

- Greeting cards
- Wide craft sticks (plain or multicolored)
- White glue
- Masking tape
- Scissors
- Curling ribbon

Tools:

- X-acto knife

Preparation (older students can do this for themselves):

- Cut the front off the greeting card.
- Save both the front picture and the inner message.
- Lay out 6 or 7 craft sticks and tape them together to hold them in position.

Activity:

- Select a greeting card picture and a message.
- Trim the card components to the desired shape and size
- Glue card picture and message to the craft sticks, masking tape side down, in any arrangement desired (note-you can easily straighten any craft sticks that shift during this process)
- Wipe off excess glue and let dry
- Optional- add personal message written directly onto the craft sticks or card

Completion:

- When completely dry, remove masking tape from the back.
- Using your X-acto knife, cut card along the craft stick "seams." (note- this is easier if you cut gently at first. Then, fold your puzzle-gram along the cut, and complete the cut all the way through)
- After completing all your cuts, tie the puzzle pieces together decoratively with the curling ribbon.

   Variation: Do not cut the puzzle-gram up. Secure a piece of yarn or ribbon to the uncut puzzle-gram to make a wall hanging.

Picture Frame—
A Sensational Gift!

(all ages/from 50 cents per project)

Materials:

Picture frame
with an inner
mat (Clearance
close out
stores are a
terrific source)

- Cardstock
  picture
  frames
  (eNasco.com)
- Wrapping paper scraps
- Pictures from Jewish catalogs and magazines
- Glue stick
- Mod Podge
- Small foam brushes
- Metallic "leafing" marker (or any other high quality marker)
- Scissors
- Tacky or other craft glue
- Sparkling "gems", buttons, tiles

Activity 1 (picture frame with mat):

- Take mat out of frame
- Using glue stick, collage wrapping paper scraps and catalog pictures to frame, covering as much area as possible.
- Fill in any empty area with the metallic or other marker
- Optional—paint over with Mod Podge but allow sufficient time for complete drying)
- Reinsert mat into frame.

Activity 2 (cardstock picture frame):

- Using glue stick, collage wrapping paper scraps and catalog pictures to frame, covering as much area as possible.
- Fill in any empty area with the metallic or other marker
- Paint carefully with Mod Podge
- Glue on gem, tile or button for decoration if desired
- Allow to dry completely

Add to the fun—use an I-Zone camera (Polaroid) to take small pictures of each student at work. Add the student's picture to the collage.

Photo Album
(pre-k and up/$1.00 per project)

Materials:

- Small photo album with a clear vinyl cover (there will be a decorative cardboard picture inside this cover)
- Catalog pictures
- Greeting cards
- Stickers/stamps and stamp pads
- Markers/colored pencils/crayons
- Scissors
- Glue stick

Preparation:

- Check to see if the reverse side of the cardboard picture insert is blank.
- If it is not blank, cut cardstock into the correct size to fit the photo album.
- Optional—have an I-Zone camera and film to photograph students at work

Activity:

- Decorate the blank cardstock or reverse side of cardboard picture insert using pictures and vocabulary that relate to the themed unit.
- Fill in any excess blank areas with marker, colored pencil or crayons as desired
- Optional—include a picture of the student at work on the cover.

- Place the cardstock in the vinyl cover
- Do remember to do both back and front covers

Switchplates And Doorhangers

(all ages/ from 25 cents per project)

These projects can be used for any theme, just like you were using construction paper. Holidays, text quotes, mitzvoth, blessings, vocabulary and more look terrific and are super gifts.

As a parent once remarked: "anyone can always find a place for a switchplate and we all have plenty of doorknobs!"

Materials:

- Switchplates and outlet covers (prices for these in plastic begin at 19 cents at home improvement stores.)
- Doorhangers (usually priced at 99cents each for wood. Watch the craft sales.) These can also be purchased as class sets, heavyweight cardstock, from eNasco.com and craft stores
- Paper scraps- wallpaper, scrapbook paper, wrapping paper, catalogs, greeting cards, tissue.
- Paint/ultra fine permanent markers/colored pencils (if using wood, you can pre-treat your wood products with a sealant if you plan to use water based markers for drawing/writing directly onto the wood)

- Mod Podge (**always test your materials first to insure that applying the Mod Podge will not smear the writing/drawing*)
- Foam brushes
- Extra collage stuff—buttons, gems, tiles, yarn
- Tacky or other craft glue
- Scissors
- Glue sticks

Tools:

- X-acto knife for carefully cutting switchplate/outlet cover openings

Preparation:

Have a selection of sources from which to draw text quotes

Activity:

- Collage/draw/paint as desired to reinforce the theme/vocabulary
- Seal with Mod Podge if desired for a more finished look (see warning above)
- Add final touches with collage extras
- Use ultra-fine permanent markers to add text quotes after Mod Podge is dry.

Wow! Doorhangers have 2 sides. Double your fun!

Banners

younger students:

Materials:

- Felt squares
- Craft glue
- Pictures from catalogs and greeting cards
- Small tubular hangers (purchase for 10cents apiece on sale)
- Optional –glitter paint/glue in a squeeze applicator
- Collage extras-gems, buttons, foam shapes, yarn bits

Preparation:

- Assemble the pictures which best reinforce your theme
- Attach felt squares to hangers by wrapping the edge of the felt around the bottom of the hanger and staple the ends to secure

Activity:

- Children glue pictures onto the banner as desired
- Optional—embellish with glitter glue/paint and collage extras
- These same banners can be made using a heavy quality paper as a base. You can also use a wood dowel instead of a hanger.

Materials:

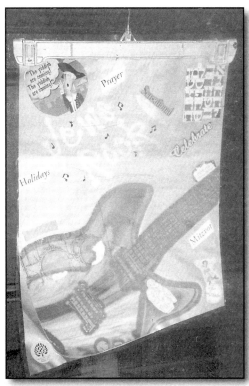

- Silk scarves
- Fabric markers/ fabric crayons
- Acrylic paint
- Small paint brushes
- Decorative stencils
- Sea sponges
- Jewish clip art or computer generated designs
- Hebrew stencils
- Scotch tape
- Simple blessings or quotes
- Plastic "skirt" hanger (purchase when on sale)

Optional preparation:

You can pre-treat your silk scarf with a scotchguard sizing and then iron in order to keep the colors from bleeding a bit. However, this extra step is generally out of keeping with a Reluctant Artist's profile. Therefore, you can simply explain to students that markers bleed a little when coloring on silk.

Mandatory Preparation:

Cover work surfaces with brown parcel paper, butcher paper or newspaper.

Activity:

- Select the patterns and blessings/quotes desired.
- Tape the patterns onto the table
- Tape the scarf onto the work surface to avoid shifting.
- Trace design onto the silk (you can use a pencil or a pale fabric marker/crayon)
- Use markers/crayons/paints to color in the design.

Or

- Tape silk to work surface
- Lay stencils on top of silk in preferred arrangement
- Tape stencils into place.
- Use sea sponge to sponge paint stencil designs onto the fabric or, trace stencil designs and complete as above.
- To facilitate writing—when writing freehand or using stencils, write your text onto a piece of white paper first. Then use the tracing technique described above.
- Outlining your designs can give a smoother finished look.
- When dry, clip your banner onto the "skirt" hanger

Extension—Hallah and Matzah Covers

You can purchase finished squares of silk fabric from **www.jacquardproducts.com**. White handkerchiefs can also be used. Paint/color as described above.

Create A Spectrum

Although this project is very simple, it is best undertaken with students 4th grade and above.

Materials

- Simple picture or stenciled text on white paper. (reproducible on next page)
- Ruler or other straight edge
- Pencil
- Markers/pastels/colored pencils

Activity:

- Select any edge of the paper from which to originate the spectrum
- Draw lines from the selected edge to the other side of the paper
- The lines must go in the same direction (side/side; up/down; diagonal) but needn't be parallel. The distance between the lines should vary. (sample below)
- Instruct students to select 2 or 3 colors with which to color, alternatively, the various spaces created by the lines intersecting with the design. Spaces can also be left white.
- Extra colors can be added for effect as desired.

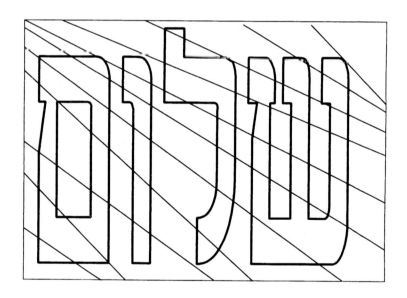

To the point

Materials:

- White paper
- Ruler or straight edge
- Hebrew stencils
- Markers/crayons/pastels/colored pencils
- List of simple Hebrew nouns (3—5 letters)

Activity:

- Select the Hebrew word to be illustrated
- Across the bottom of the page, draw a square for each
  Hebrew letter

- Stencil or draw a letter in each box (to spell the word). Try to fill the box with the letter.
- Find a center point on the paper, approximately one third of the way down from the top edge.
- With the straight edge, draw lines from the top of each square, converging on the center point.
- At the point of convergence, draw a picture which illustrates the meaning of the vocabulary word selected.

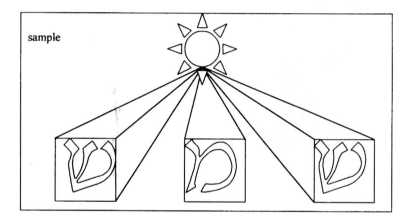

Take Half

(kdg on up)

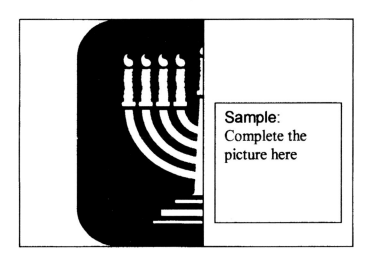

Sample:
Complete the
picture here

Materials:

- Pictures from Jewish calendars (for older students)
- Simple Jewish shape or picture (younger students)
- White paper
- Markers/crayons/pastels/colored pencils
- Book of Jewish quotes (optional)
- Fine line gel pen (optional)
- Scissors
- Glue stick

Preparation:

- Cut pictures in half or into two uneven pieces

- Glue your ½ picture onto the white paper, either to the left or right of center depending on the picture's correct orientation)

Activity:

- Have students select the ½ picture that pleases them.
- Instruct students to complete the picture in whatever way they feel best.
- Encourage them to look carefully at the Judaic elements of the picture they have selected.
- Remind them that their goal is to create an original piece of art; not to exactly replicate the original picture.

  • optional conclusion: for more abstract pictures, students may wish to use a fine line gel pen to inscribe a meaningful quote.

Pyramid

(1st grade and above)

Preparation:

- Reproduce the Pyramid pattern (below) onto white cardstock. (can be enlarged)
- Select a theme which can be organized into 3 parts:
  - T'shuvah/tzedakah/t'fillah
  - Meat/dairy/pareve
  - Torah/devotion/acts of loving, kindness

Materials:

- Markers/crayons/colored pencils
- Thematic pictures from magazines or newspapers (optional)
- Glue issors

Activity:

- Brainstorm aspects of the areas you are studying
- Students label each third of the pyramid
- Instruct students to illustrate each theme
- Glue the pyramid as indicated to complete.
- Do not decorate

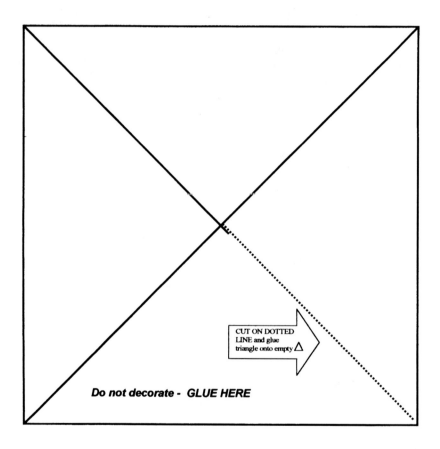

CUT ON DOTTED LINE and glue triangle onto empty △

Do not decorate - GLUE HERE

woven Mizrah

(4th grade and up)

Materials:

- 2 pieces of cardstock cut to the desired size (minimum of 6" X 6") (construction paper can be used also)
- Hebrew stencil (or cut out letters מזרח)
- Markers
- Glue stick

Teacher Tool:

- X-acto blade
- scissors

Preparation:

- With X-acto blade, cut lines across the weaving base, leaving ¼ inch margin on either side (figure A). Use a ruler if you wish to measure exactly and have straight lines. Irregular lines are attractive as well.

- Take a second piece of paper to cut the weaving strips. Cut these strips in the opposite direction of the cuts on the weaving base. Cut this paper from end to end to achieve separate strips (figure B) These strips can be of any width. Again you can use a ruler for exact measurement and straight lines or you can cut casually)

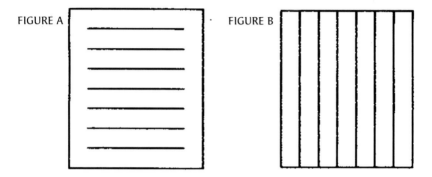

FIGURE A · FIGURE B

Activity:

- Acquaint your students in weaving a strip **over/*under*/over** and demonstrate the next strip weaving ***under*/over/*under*** (do not assume they are familiar with the technique).
- Instruct the students to continue in this fashion until the weaving mat is complete.
- Advise students to secure loose ends with the glue stick.
- Use the stencil, or draw "bubble letters" free-hand, to write the word מזרח on the woven mat
- Use marker(s) to color *either* the letters *or* the woven squares around the letters.

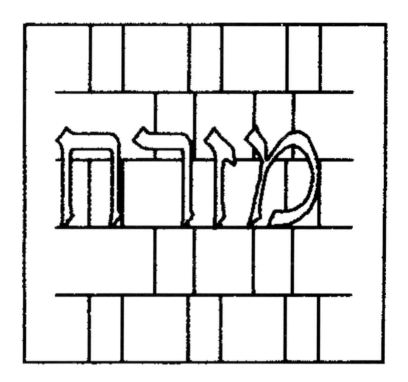

Extensions:

- Punch holes at the edges; fringe with yarn and beads.
- Tie tzit-tzit in a corner.
- Before preparing the weaving mats/strips, copy designs or suitable blessings onto the cardstock you will be weaving.
- Have students write Hebrew or English quotes, blessings or vocabulary onto the cut weaving strips and then weave as above.
- Embellish with stickers

Quilt It!

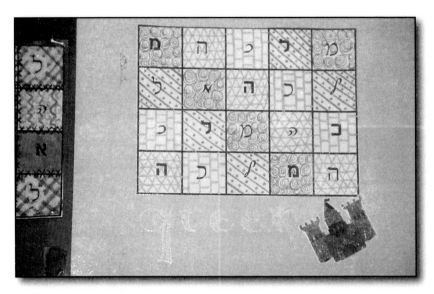

Materials:

- "Quilt" pattern copied (enlarge if desired) onto white paper (cardstock is preferable)
- Hebrew stencils and/or English stencils
- Markers or colored pencils
- Students' Hebrew names or vocabulary to be reinforced

Activity:

- Instruct students to write their Hebrew name or the selected vocabulary word onto the quilt pattern, one letter per square. (use stencils or the "bubble" technique -
- draw your letter as usual, lightly with pencil. Outline your letter all around to nlarge it. Erase the initial "stick" letter which is in the middle of the "bubble" letter. Works for Hebrew and English)

- Repeat the word continuously until you can no longer write out the word in its entirety. (never end in the middle of the word simply because you have run out of quilt squares)

  In any remaining squares, illustrate the name/word, write its translation or write related themes.

Instruct students to decorate each letter square with a doodle (appropriately thematic if possible), using the same doodle repeatedly for each identical letter.

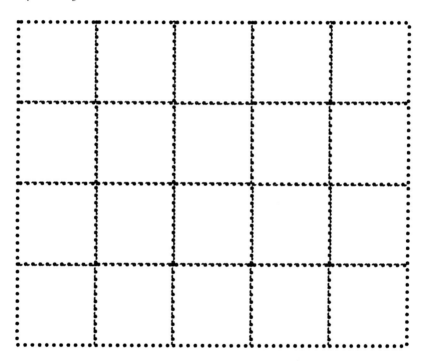

ADD PIZZAZZ TO YOUR PAPER PROJECTS!

Ask your local wallpaper distributor to call you when there are outdated books available.

- When your project calls for gluing construction paper, try substituting wallpaper in patterns of the desired color. Magazine pictures, cut randomly according to color, work well also.

- Create mosaic squares easily by using a paper cutter to cut wallpaper pieces into the size squares you desire.
- Stripes, cut from wallpaper borders, serve wonderfully as frames and borders for art and reports.

Purchase a Hebrew newspaper from your local Judaica store!

- One newspaper should be enough to last for the entire year.
- Use the newspaper (especially the want ads) as an art background. Color in the ad squares with marker or colored pencil.
- Create geometric collages, mixing colors, fonts and shapes cut from the paper.
- Use the newspaper as an alternative to construction paper pieces whenever you might otherwise gluing shapes or stripes onto a construction paper background.

Become a word Artist!

Illustrate the meaning of a word as you write it. Separate the letters of the word *havdalah*; create a lightening bolt with *barak*, use a rainbow design to illustrate *keshet*.

Link It!

Have a lengthy list to study? Write each detail on an individual paper strip (construction paper works best); decorate each strip and link them together to adorn your classroom. A fun alternative to a time line.

placemats are perfect!

Purchase inexpensive white placemats at restaurant supply or clearance outlets. Have students use markers, colored pencils or crayons to decorate the embossed designs. Add the blessing or message you are teaching and laminate or seal in clear contac paper. Just right for candle drip mats or halla<u>h</u> trays.

wear it!

Have students illustrate their lesson on a sentence strip. Encourage lots of color and add stickers. When complete, punch a hole in either end, thread yarn and have a belt or a banner to wear.

Bayit Blessings

(5th grade and up/
$1.50 per student)

Materials:

- Straw brooms (buy on seasonal sales at craft store or at clearance close-out store)
- Artificial flowers or leaves
- Ribbon
- Hole punch
- Yarn
- Scissors
- Tacky or other craft glue
- Cardstock or index cards
- Gel Pens or fine tip markers
- Blessings or quotes referring to family and home life

Preparation:

Review the concept of *Shalom Bayit* with your students.

Activity:

- Using the Tacky or craft glue, decorate the broom with the artificial foliage and the ribbon.
- Set the broom aside to dry.

- Select a quote or blessing which is particularly meaningful to you.
- Carefully copy your selected quote onto a small piece of cardstock or an index card, leaving enough space at the top to punch a hole
- Decorate the cardstock/index card as desired
- Punch a hole in the center top of the blessing card.
- Using narrow ribbon or yarn, tie the blessing card onto the broom so it rests decoratively on the foliage. Secure card with a dab of glue.

> "Each child brings his/her own blessing into the world"
> —Yiddish saying

> "What the child says outdoors, s/he has learned indoors"
> —Talmud

> "To be rooted is perhaps the most important and least recognized need of the human soul"
> —Simone Weil

> "Say little and do much"
> —Talmud

> "That's what life is: a collection of rare and unusual moments, like an array of gems set out before you"
> —Sarah Bernhard

> "One does not get better, but different and older and that is always a pleasure"
> —Gertrude Stein

Blessing Baskets

(kdg and up/ $1.00 per project)

This project makes wonderful gifts for a respite center or nursing home.

Materials:

- Small baskets (purchase these on seasonal sales or at clearance close-out stores)
- Artificial flowers and leaves
- Styrofoam blocks (these can be cut from used packing materials)
- Index cards or cardstock
- Small flower stickers
- Gel pens or thin line markers
- Craft glue
- Plastic forks
- Blessings for the season or for peace

Preparation:

- Cut Styrofoam to fit inside the baskets
- Place a piece of Styrofoam in each basket

Activity:

- Select a basket
- Place a plastic fork, tines up, in the front center of the styrofoam.
- Arrange artificial flowers and leaves around the fork.
- Secure with dabs of glue when necessary.
- Copy a blessing carefully onto a piece of cardstock/index card
- Or copy, cut and paste a blessing onto the cardstock/index card.
- Decorate the blessing card with stickers or small drawings
- Carefully place the blessing card between the times of the fork.

  Alternative: place recipe cards in the fork

Holiday Blessing—
Project & Recipe Pots

(3rd grade and up/ 75cents per project)

Materials:

- 3 inch clay pots (leave the sticker on the bottom)
- paint
- Catalog pictures for the holiday/theme to be reinforced
- Mod Podge
- Foam brushes
- Sea sponge
- Quick setting Plaster of Paris
- Stirring sticks (craft sticks/ chop sticks)
- Plastic forks
- Dried flowers
- Water
- Glue stick
- Index cards

Preparation:

- Determine the focus of your lesson.

- Depending upon the area to be reinforced photocopy blessing(s), recipe(s), or ritual(s) pertinent to your subject.
- Have students, parents or aides glue these onto index cards
- Be certain that each clay pot has a sticker covering the bottom hole. If not, place a small piece of masking tape over the hole.

Activity:

- Paint the clay pot as desired using foam brushes or sea sponges.
- Glue catalog picture(s) to pot to illustrate theme.
- Cover pot with Mod Podge using either foam brushes, sea sponges or hands.
- Set pot aside to dry <u>overnight.</u>
- Carefully scoop Plaster of Paris powder into clay pot.
- Add water and stir to a "pudding like" consistency.
- Test to see when fork can stand (tines up) in the middle of the pot, unsupported. [this will hold the index card(s)]
- Insert dried flowers into the plaster surrounding the fork

Conclusion

Place index card(s) into the tines of the fork

Drum Roll

(pre-K and above/ 40 cents per project)

Makes classroom music into an entertainment delight!

Materials:

- Container of salt (go for the cheapest kind)
- Paper scraps (wrapping paper, scrapbook paper, comic strips, tissue paper)
- Glue stick
- Masking tape
- Mod Podge (have pie tins available for Mod Podge)
- Foam brushes or sponges
- Crayons or markers

Preparation:

- Empty approximately ¾ of the salt into a separate container. Save the salt (see instructions below)
- Use masking tape to tape the spout securely shut
- Pour Mod Podge into pie tins

Activity:

- Instruct the students to cover the entire "drum" with colorful scraps of paper.
- Students can color in any empty spaces with the crayons or markers.
- Cover the entire drum with Mod Podge (apply either with foam brushes, sponges or fingers)

Conclusion:

Set the drums to the side to dry and explain to the students that they cannot play them until they are totally dry.

After the students go home, reapply Mod Podge to each drum to insure a solid coat.

Play!

Use the drums as percussion or as shakers each time your class has music.

Save the Salt! Place the salt into small jars and mix each with powdered, colored, tempera paint. Use this as craft sand for collages or paper weights.

Shakers!

(3rd grade and up; minimal cost per student)

Materials:

- Small containers (with lids/not glass) of any and every kind. (request donations from families or, ask a local photo shop for empty film canisters)
- Inexpensive book of Jewish piano music or song music
- Or find all those old Jewish song sheets you have been collecting for years.
- Scissors
- Glue sticks
- Colored pencils (watercolor pencils are especially terrific for this)
- Mod Podge (the sparkle Mod Podge adds a special touch)
- Small foam brushes
- Items for sound—rice; small paper clips; whole cloves; small pebbles; seeds etc.
- Sharpie Marker (optional)

Activity:

- Instruct students to put several "sound" items into their container to create the sound they prefer.
- Place the cover securely on the shaker.
- Cut the music/song sheets into small pieces of various shapes.
- Color the music sheet pieces you have selected.

- Use the music sheet pieces and the glue sticks to cover your container completely.
- If desired, use Sharpie marker to carefully outline the shapes of the paper pieces on the container.
- Cover the shaker with Mod Podge using a small foam brush or fingers.
- Place shakers on wax paper to dry. Touch up any places that have escaped the Mod Podge cover.

Mezzuzot For All Ages

younger students

Materials:

- One piece of Fun Foam, heavy cardstock, or lightweight wood per student
- Stickers; calendar cut outs; or borders representing hands, hearts, houses, gates
- Sparkling "gem" (optional)
- White glue
- Wiggly eyes
- Double stick mounting squares or picture hanger

Preparation:

Depending on the focus of your lesson, ask students to write or illustrate their own version of "You shall love..." or, have a simple version preprinted for them.

Activity:

Children can collage their "mezuzah" freely incorporating each element.

Finish with a single sparkling "gem" if desired.

Conclusion:

Place mounting squares or picture hanger on the back of each mezuzah.

Middle years students

Materials:

- Used rolls from a cash register (ask a friendly neighborhood merchant to save used cash register rolls for you)
- Or Prefolded coin wrapper rolls
- Masking tape
- Scraps of tissue paper or wrapping paper
- Or selected clip art designs
- Colored pencils (if using clip art)
- Wide craft sticks
- Tacky or other craft glue
- Mod Podge
- Sparkling "Gems"
- Double stick mounting tabs

Preparation:

Have each student write their own version of the *V'ahavta* on lightweight paper or, provide a scroll for each student

Activity:

- Wrap the plastic cash register roll in masking tape (this creates a surface which is "glue friendly.")
- Decorate the roll with tissue and wrapping paper scraps
- Or color clip art/original design
- If using clip art/original design, glue design onto the cash register roll/coin roll
- Cover the bottom of the roll
- Place scroll inside the roll and cover the top.
- Mod Podge the entire roll to give it a finished glaze.

Note: original artwork should <u>not</u> be Mod Podged unless you are absolutely certain it can take this without streaking.

- Glue the finished roll to the craft stick using a strong craft glue –this will require that the student hold it in place for a bit of time or, you can cheat with double stick tape or mounting tabs.
- Decorate with a sparkling "gem" if desired.
- Affix with double stick mounting tabs

Middle to Older Students

Materials:

- Shop in your craft store for any kind of tiny wood, basket or pottery flower holder that is wall mountable.
- Vellum or other sheer paper
- Dried flowers
- Fine point gel ink pen
- Ribbon
- Double stick mounting tabs or small nail

Preparation:

- Collect a selection of siddurim as well as alternative liturgy with a variety of wordings for the *V'ahavta*.
- Consider the type of decorative touches—paint, stickers, etc., which would enhance your flower holders.

Activity:

- Decorate the flower holder as desired.
- Each student should create a personal *V'ahavta* on a small piece of vellum paper.
- Roll the paper and tie with a piece of slender ribbon
- Place the scroll in the flower holder
- Add dry flowers
- Affix with mounting tabs or a small nail

Tzedakah Bag

early elementary

Materials:

- Drawstring bag (heavy plastic—generally found in close-out stores or "surplus")
- Blank diskette labels
- Crayons/markers/colored pencils
- Clear Contac® paper
- Shiny Star of David stickers

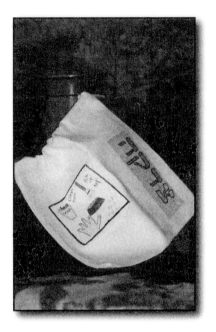

Preparation:

- Reproduce and cut tzedakah labels (on facing page)
- Cut Contac® paper to a size somewhat larger than tzedakah labels
- Place 1 or 2 diskette labels on each side of the bag

Activity:

- Discuss the importance of tzedakah and brainstorm chores children can do to earn money at home.
- Instruct children to illustrate possible jobs on diskette labels (alternative designs can include coins or dollars, or any favorite design.
- Have children decorate the tzedakah label.

- **Teacher**—place completed tzedakah label **face down** onto the **sticky** side of clear Contac® paper.
- Place tzedakah label onto bag (if using "surplus" product, cover any existing labeling)

Conclusion:

- When the project has been finished carefully, offer each student two shiny Star of David (or other) stickers to enhance the tzedakah bag.
- Review the goal to do chores at home and bring tzedakah back to school in the bag.
- Include a note to parents to encourage parents to help their children earn tzedakah money.

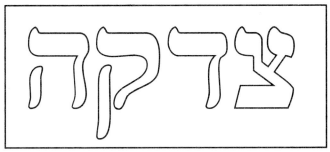

Beyond Tzedakah

(pre-kdg and above)

Tzedakah Boxes

You can purchase paper machè boxes in all shapes and sizes at your local craft retailer. These are frequently on sale. If you wish, use your X-acto knife to cut a slit for coins in the cover. Wood boxes are also available at craft stores but are more costly. Children's pencil boxes are inexpensive at back to school time.

Paint the box if desired. If you are using pencil boxes that are already patterned, you can add white glue to your tempera paint. This will add to the quality of the paint coverage.

Using Mod Podge as an adhesive, you can add wrapping paper pieces, newspaper strips, collage pictures or stickers to embellish the box.

Always add a sparkling gem for the perfect finish!

Energize Your Art Program

Offer art "menu options." Not all students need to do the same project at the same time. This method will also help use up craft odds and ends.

Art need not be driven by the calendar. Incorporate Hebrew, values, text and history. Look at secular teaching resource books and make the leap to your curriculum.

Bring Judaism home. Look around your home at the items you use all the time. In class, paint dishtowels; create a tray for the TV remote; make magnets for the refrigerator or a cover for the tissues. Put Jewish symbols and text all around your students' homes.

Always do your project at home first to work out any kinks. However, you do not need to show a completed sample unless you students request to see one. Give your students some basic parameters to cover your content goal and let them go their own route.

Try to have one concluding component to each project that is extra special—a sparkling gem; glow in the dark paint; a gold or silver leafing pen. Or, incorporate a supply that will be used for this one project only—tile pieces; parchment paper; puzzle pieces.

Coordinate your supply shopping to take advantage of bulk discounts. Shop the "stock up" sales and take advantage of coupon saving to purchase specialty supplies.

Store project leftovers in a community closet so that they can be used by other teachers. Keep the closet tidy so that all supplies can be seen and used.

Coordinate your projects with other teachers. There is a limit to how many matzah covers one family can use. Diversify so that one class makes the matzah covers, another the kiddush cup, another ḥaroset bowl, etc.

Now and again, put out a supply item "just because." You may not know what to do with it but your kids will!